NEIGHBORHOOD HELPERS

Teachers

BY CECILIA MINDEN

The Child's World

Content Adviser:
Simin H. Rasmussen,
Program Advisor,
Department of Teacher
Education, Northeastern
Illinois University,
Chicago, Illinois

Published in the United States of America by The Child's World®
PO Box 326
Chanhassen, MN 55317-0326
800-599-READ
www.childsworld.com

Acknowledgements

The Child's World®: Mary Berendes, Publishing Director

Editorial Directions, Inc.: E. Russell Primm, Editorial Director; Katie Marsico, Managing Editor and Line Editor; Judith Shiffer, Assistant Editor; Caroline Wood, Editorial Assistant; Susan Hindman, Copy Editor; Wendy Mead, Proofreader; Mike Helenthal, Rory Mabin, and Caroline Wood, Fact Checkers; Tim Griffin/IndexServ, Indexer; Cian Loughlin O'Day, Photo Researcher; Linda S. Koutris, Photo Selector

The Design Lab: Kathleen Petelinsek, Design and Art Production

Photographs ©: Cover: left—RubberBall Productions, right/frontispiece—Brand X Pictures. Interior: 4—Photodisc/Getty Images; 5—RubberBall Productions; 6, 13, 15, 21, 28-left, 28-right—Brand X Pictures; 7—Seth Joel/Taxi/Getty Images; 8-9—Digital Vision/Getty Images; 11, 23—Stewart Cohen/Taxi/Getty Images; 12, 20—Cindy Chiu; 14-15—Najlah Feanny/Corbis; 16-17—Superstock/Alamy Images; 19—LWA/JDC/Corbis; 24-25—Jeff Greenberg/Photo Edit; 26-27—Jim Cummins/Taxi/Getty Images.

Library of Congress Cataloging-in-Publication Data

Minden, Cecilia.
  Teachers / by Cecilia Minden.
      p. cm. — (Neighborhood helpers)
  ISBN 1-59296-569-5 (library bound : alk. paper)
  1. Teachers—Juvenile literature. I. Title. II. Series.
  LB1775.M625 2006
  371.1—dc22   2005026218

TABLE OF CONTENTS

Hello. My name is Maria. Many people live and work in my neighborhood. Each of them helps the neighborhood in different ways.

I thought of all the things I like to do. I like to go to school. I like helping others learn new skills.

How could I help my neighborhood when I grow up?

When Did This Job Start?

The first school in the United States to train new teachers opened in 1823. It was in Concord, Vermont. Nearly every state had such schools by 1900. Today, almost every university has a school of education to train new teachers.

I COULD BE A TEACHER!

Teachers enjoy learning. They know a lot about many different subjects. Teachers are good at helping students build new skills.

Best of all, teachers get to help others learn!

Do you like helping others learn?
Perhaps you'd make a good teacher!

COMPOSITION

100 sheets • 200 pages
9¾ x 7½ in/24.7 x 19.0 cm
wide ruled

$$\frac{\partial^2 v}{\partial x^2} + \frac{\partial^2 v}{\partial y^2} + \frac{\partial^2 v}{\partial z^2} = -u$$

$$\frac{1}{2\pi} \int_0^{2\pi} u(\phi) \overline{a^2 - 2}$$

or, for $\zeta = ae^{i\phi}$ and $z = re^{i\phi}$

$$\frac{1}{2\pi} \int_0^{2\pi} \operatorname{Re}\left(\frac{\zeta + z}{\zeta - z}\right) u(\phi$$

the value at the point x
of the function which is har

LEARN ABOUT THIS NEIGHBORHOOD HELPER!

The best way to learn is to ask questions. Words such as *who*, *what*, *where*, *when*, and *why* will help me learn about being a teacher.

Asking your teacher questions will help you learn more about his job.

Where Can I Learn More?

National Association
for the Education of
Young Children
1509 16th Street NW
Washington, DC 20036

Recruiting New
Teachers, Inc.
385 Concord Avenue
Suite 103
Belmont, MA 02478

How Can I Explore This Job?

Ask your teacher about her job! Where did he go to school? How did he decide to become a teacher? What does he like best about teaching?

WHO CAN BECOME A TEACHER?

Girls and boys who enjoy learning and helping others may want to become teachers. There are many different kinds of teachers. They help others learn from kindergarten all the way through college.

Teachers are important helpers in the neighborhood. They teach people how to read, write, solve problems, and learn new skills.

Teachers help people of all ages learn new skills.

MEET A TEACHER!

This is Cindy Chiu. Her students call her Miss Chiu. She is a reading teacher at a school in Arlington, Virginia. Miss Chiu teaches children how to become better readers and writers. When Miss Chiu is not in the classroom, she likes to swim, play tennis, read books, and write in her journal.

Miss Chiu enjoys helping her students learn how to read.

How Many Teachers Are There?

About 3,800,000 people work as teachers.

WHERE CAN I LEARN TO BE A TEACHER?

Teachers usually go to college. They take classes in many subjects because they have to help students learn many different things. Most teachers have to take a special test to get a teaching license. Teachers never stop learning. They sometimes take classes in the summer while students are on vacation!

Teachers usually take a variety of college classes.

How Much School Will I Need?

Public school teachers must have a four-year college degree. They must also take teacher training classes. Many states require education past college. Teachers must pass tests given by the state where they live. They are then given a license so they can work.

Books

Computer

Dry erase board and markers

Internet

Paper

Pen or pencil

dry erase board (DRYE i-RAYSS BORD) a board covered with white, glossy plastic that can be written on with markers and later wiped clean

WHAT DOES A TEACHER NEED TO DO HER JOB?

Miss Chiu loves books! She has many books for her students to read. Miss Chiu often uses a **dry erase board** when she is teaching.

Sometimes Miss Chiu's students have writing projects. She asks them to share what they write. Students take turns sitting in a chair called the Author's Chair. There they read what they wrote to the other children in the class.

Books are an important part of most classrooms.

What Clothes Will I Wear?

For men:
Dress shirt or sweater
Slacks

For women:
Blouse or sweater
Slacks

It is helpful for both men and women teachers to wear comfortable shoes.

What's It Like Where I'll Work?

Teachers usually work in classrooms. These are clean and well-lighted. Sometimes teachers work outdoors. They watch children on the playground and during outdoor field trips.

WHERE DOES A TEACHER WORK?

Miss Chiu's school has several classrooms, a gym for sports, and a playground for recess. There is also a computer lab and a library stacked with books for the children to read.

Miss Chiu usually comes to school early in the morning. She meets with other teachers to think of fun activities for the students. Miss Chiu meets with

Many schools feature computer labs.

younger students later in the morning. She teaches these students how to read.

Miss Chiu works with older children in the afternoon. They already know how to read. She helps them to become better readers. The students leave in the afternoon, but most teachers stay after school to attend meetings and to get their classroom ready for the next day.

Miss Chiu helps both younger and older children develop their reading skills.

How Much Money Will I Make?

Most teachers make between $40,000 and $45,000 a year.

What Other Jobs Might I Like?

Librarian

Library media specialist

Principal

Recreation worker

Teacher's aide

WHO WORKS WITH TEACHERS?

Many people work with Miss Chiu at school. They include a principal, a librarian, a nurse, a coach, a secretary, a bus driver, a **custodian,** volunteers, and others who want to help the students learn.

custodian (kuhss-TOH-dee-uhn)
someone who cleans a building and helps take care of it

Librarians and teachers work together to show students that reading can be fun.

WHEN IS A TEACHER A DIRECTOR?

Teachers are always working, but their work doesn't always take place inside a classroom. They often help students with **extracurricular** activities. Miss Chiu and her students like to perform in a Reader's Theater. The students choose a favorite book and make a play using the characters from the book. They practice and practice. They like to perform their play for family and friends. Miss Chiu uses a video camera to make a tape of the play. She sends a copy of the tape home to parents who were not able to come to the play.

Miss Chiu uses some of her free time to help students perform in a Reader's Theater.

How Might My Job Change?

Some teachers go on to become principals, counselors, and library media specialists.

extracurricular (ek-struh-kuh-RIK-yuh-luhr) student activities that occur after school or that don't make up the main part of a child's studies

Is This Job Growing?

The need for teachers will grow as fast as other jobs.

I WANT TO BE A TEACHER!

I think being a teacher would be a great way to be a neighborhood helper. Someday you may see me at the front of a classroom!

Raise your hand if you know the answer! Maybe one day you'll be helping kids in your neighborhood learn.

WHY DON'T YOU TRY BEING A TEACHER?

Do you think you would like to be a teacher? Why don't you create a how-to book? How-to books have instructions that show people how to do different things. You could teach someone how to tell a joke, make a peanut butter sandwich, jump rope, or whatever you know how to do.

Materials: pencils, crayons, markers, paper, stapler

Steps:

1. Think about something you can teach others.
2. Make a list of all the materials you need.
3. Write out the instructions, step by step. You may have to do this several times until you are sure the directions are very clear.
4. Copy each step of the instructions on a separate paper.
5. Draw a picture for each step to show the reader what to do.
6. Put the pictures and instructions, in order, between two pieces of colorful paper and staple them together.

I Didn't Know That!

Anne Sullivan (1866–1936) was a famous teacher who helped one of her students overcome several challenges. Anne taught Helen Keller (1880–1968), a little girl who was both blind and deaf. Anne worked with Helen and showed her how to use sign language to speak. Helen also became famous over time. She and Anne remained good friends for the rest of their lives.

HOW TO LEARN MORE ABOUT TEACHERS

BOOKS

Hayward, Linda. *A Day in the Life of a Teacher.* New York: Dorling Kindersley, 2001.

Liebman, Daniel. *I Want to Be a Teacher.* Toronto: Firefly Books, 2001.

Parks, Peggy J. *Teacher.* Farmington Hills, Mich.: Kidhaven Press, 2003.

Simon, Charnan. *Teachers.* Chanhassen, Minn.: The Child's World, 2003.

Vogel, Elizabeth. *Meet My Teacher.* New York: PowerKids Press, 2002.

WEB SITES

Visit our home page for lots of links about teachers:
http://www.childsworld.com/links

Note to Parents, Teachers, and Librarians:

We routinely check our Web links to make sure they're safe, active sites—so encourage your readers to check them out!

ABOUT THE AUTHOR:

Dr. Cecilia Minden is a university professor and reading specialist with classroom and administrative experience in grades K-12. She is the author of many books for early readers. Cecilia and her husband Dave Cupp live in North Carolina.

INDEX